IN PRAISE OF EDWARD DE BONO

'Edward doesn't just think. He is a one-man global industry, whose work is gospel in government, universities, schools, corporates and even prisons all over the world' *Times 2*

'The master of creative thinking' *Independent on Sunday*

'Edward de Bono is a cult figure in developing tricks to sharpen the mind' *The Times*

'Edward de Bono is a toolmaker, his tools have been fashioned for thinking, to make more of the mind' Peter Gabriel

'de Bono's work may be the best thing going in the world today' George Gallup, originator of the Gallup Poll

'The guru of clear thinking' *Marketing Week*

www.edwarddebono.com

ALSO BY EDWARD DE BONO FROM VERMILION

SIX FRAMES
For Thinking about Information

Edward de Bono

Vermilion
LONDON

1 3 5 7 9 10 8 6 4 2

Published in 2008 by Vermilion, an imprint of Ebury Publishing

Ebury Publishing is a Random House Group company

Copyright © McQuaig Group Inc. 2008

Edward de Bono has asserted his moral right to be identified as
the author of this Work in accordance with the Copyright, Design
and Patents Act 1988.

The Random House Group Limited Reg. No. 954009

Addresses for companies within the Random House Group can be
found at www.rbooks.co.uk

A CIP catalogue record for this book is available from the British
Library

The Random House Group Limited supports The Forest
Stewardship Council (FSC), the leading international forest
certification organisation. All our titles that are printed on
Greenpeace-approved FSC-certified paper carry the FSC logo.
Our paper procurement policy can be found at
www.rbooks.co.uk/environment

Mixed Sources
Product group from well-managed
forests and other controlled sources
www.fsc.org Cert no. TT-COC-2139
© 1996 Forest Stewardship Council
FSC

Printed and bound in Great Britain by
CPI Mackays, Chatham, ME5 8TD

ISBN: 9780091924195

Copies are available at special rates for bulk orders. Contact the
sales development team on 020 7840 8487 for more information.

To buy books by your favourite authors and register for offers,
visit www.rbooks.co.uk

CONTENTS

PREFACE

Attention is a very key part of thinking. Yet we pay very little attention to attention itself. It is assumed that it just happens.

Attention can be pulled or attracted to something unusual. If you saw someone lying in the road, your attention would go to that person. If you saw a bright pink dog, your attention, and your sympathy, would go to that dog.

That is precisely the weakness of attention. It is pulled to the unusual. How much attention do we pay to the usual?

Perception is a key part of thinking. Research by David Perkins at Harvard has shown that ninety per cent of errors of thinking were errors of perception. No amount of excellent logic will make up for errors of perception. Goedel's theorem shows that from within a situation no amount of logic can prove the starting points, which remain arbitrary perceptions.

Attention is a key element of perception. Without the ability to direct attention, we see only the familiar patterns.

DIRECTING ATTENTION

What can we do about attention? Instead of waiting for our attention to be pulled towards something unusual, we can set out frameworks for 'directing' our attention in a conscious manner.

Just as we can decide to look north or south-east, so we can set up a framework for directing our attention. That is what the Six Frames are all about. Each frame is a direction in which to look. We look and then notice, and note what we see in that direction.

In this way we can look for need satisfaction. We can look for value. We can look for interest. We can look for accuracy, etc. Each of the Six Frames is used to direct our attention.

MASSES OF INFORMATION

We are surrounded by information. It has never been easier to obtain information (the internet, etc.) But information by itself is not enough. It is how we look at the information that matters. How do we get the most value from the information? That is an area that needs attention.

The Six Frames provide a method for extracting more value from information. They are therefore as important as the information itself.

The method is very simple to use. To be effective, however, it is essential to be deliberate and disciplined. Just to believe you are doing something is not as good as doing that thing formally and deliberately.

Introduction

The big enemy of good thinking is confusion.

Unfortunately, the more active the mind, the greater the risk of confusion. The aim of all good thinking is clarity. But clarity is no good if it is at the expense of comprehensiveness. To be very clear about a tiny part of the situation is no good at all – and even dangerous. There is a need to obtain clarity and comprehensiveness at the same time.

The main cause of confusion is trying to do everything at once. When the mind tries to do everything at once, the mind ends up doing one thing thoroughly and other things hardly at all. That is why my Six Thinking Hats is such a powerful framework. In a discussion, if we try to do everything at once we end up in the negative and critical mode because this is the easiest mode and the one we use most often. The Six Hats is now very widely used, even at top economic meetings, because it ensures a thorough exploration of the subject and a discussion that is constructive.

We live in an information age. We are bombarded by information and we have easy access to as much information as we need – in fact much more than we need. How do we react to that information?

If you have a very specific need for information and a very specific question that needs an answer, then you go to the right place and get the answer. If you need to find a flight from London to Paris that leaves London as soon as possible after six in the evening, you go to an airline timetable or ask your travel agent. There is still some thinking to be done regarding your choice of airport and airline. The traffic on the road to Heathrow is likely to be very heavy at that time.

If we only dealt with information that we really needed, life would be simpler but very limited and very dull. We also need to react to the information that we come across on television and radio and in newspapers, magazines and other people's conversations. How do we react to that information?

There are many important aspects of information, such as accuracy, bias, interest, relevance, value, etc. We could seek to assess these different aspects all at once. We could also separate them out to avoid confusion and to make sure that we cover all the different ways of looking at the information.

That is what *Six Frames For Thinking about Information* seeks to do. We look through one frame at a time. How accurate is this information? What bias is there in the information? The Six Frames are laid out in this book.

You can get into the habit of using the frames yourself. You can deliberately direct your attention to one or other frame. You can ask someone else to use a particular frame: 'Try the Square Frame on this. What do you see?' The frames can also be used in a discussion where everyone adopts the same frame at a given moment.

If you ask someone to go out into the garden and look at all the colours, that person is likely to notice the dominant colours – red in roses, yellow in daffodils, etc. – but may not notice colours that are less obvious. If you asked the same person to go out and look for the colour blue, and then the colour red and then the colour yellow, the attention scan would be much more comprehensive.

Having frames for thinking about information means that with each frame the mind is prepared and sensitised to notice different things. We can pay attention to the accuracy of the information. We can pay attention to the point of view expressed in the information. We can pay attention to the interest in the information. Each frame prepares the mind to look at the information in a specific way. We see what we are prepared to see.

The Six Frames described in this book provide a simple tool for experiencing and looking at information.

There is an unexpected outcome when the Six Thinking Hats are used. The framework might seem to complicate discussions and make them much longer. In fact, use of the Hats reduces meeting time to a quarter or even a tenth. In the same way, the Six Frames greatly simplify the way we look at information instead of complicating it. Doing one thing at a time is simpler than trying to do many things and worrying that we might be leaving out something important.

As you read through this book, keep the image of each frame clearly in mind. This image becomes the trigger symbol for each of the six ways we need to think about information. At times we may choose to focus on one way of thinking about information rather than another. That now becomes a deliberate choice.

By separating out the different ways of thinking about information and by symbolising these different ways as frames of various shapes, we take control of the way our mind performs. We can now direct our attention more deliberately rather than letting it wander in its own confused way.

We know that perception is the most important part of thinking. So the way we perceive information is all-important.

1

PURPOSE

The Triangle Frame

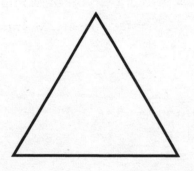

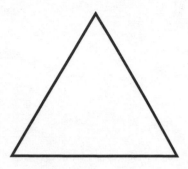

Triangles have points. A long horizontal triangle suggests an arrow pointing in a particular direction. That direction is the purpose. With the Triangle Frame, we consider the purpose of our looking at information.

We are surrounded by information all the time. Much of that time we do not have an 'information purpose'. Some of the time we do. It is useful to have a clear idea of that purpose.

NOTICE

You are walking down the road to the supermarket to buy some breakfast cereal. That is your clear

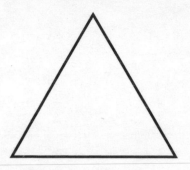

purpose. You notice a poster that is upside down. This catches your eye. You wonder whether it was carelessness or whether it was deliberately placed that way to catch attention – as it has caught your attention.

You notice a shop window that has a very bright display made up entirely of purple clothes. This has caught your attention, as it was designed to do.

Something catches our attention and we look at it. We notice it.

We can wait for our attention to be pulled or attracted to something – or we can direct our attention. The two are not exclusive. We can choose

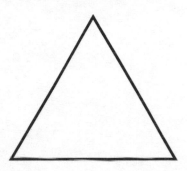

to direct our attention and still be open to having our attention pulled towards something.

Directing attention is an act of will. You can direct your attention as you might direct the beam of a searchlight.

As you walk along to the supermarket you can choose to notice the colour of the façades of all the little shops on the way. Is there any consistency? Do all tobacconists use the same colour? Is there a colour-coding or is it up to the artistic preference of the owner? Which colour seems to attract attention best? Maybe some colours are easier to keep looking fresh and clean?

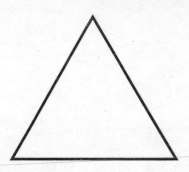

You can choose to direct your attention to the shoes of the passers-by. Are these practical walking shoes that might be worn all day? Do the shoes indicate the possible income status of their owner? You can choose to notice whether shoes are clean or not. Does this reflect the general appearance of the rest of the person?

Whenever you choose to direct your attention in a particular way, there are always questions and speculations that follow your notice. You may seek to make generalisations. You may observe exceptions to your generalisations.

Where you choose to direct your attention and what you choose to notice is up to you. If you are

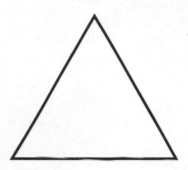

playing this game, however, you should be able to spell out clearly what you have chosen to notice. By choosing to notice things, you pull from the world around you information that has not been prepared and presented to you.

TIME-FILLING AND DISTRACTION

Much of the time we look at information as a way of filling time and as a distraction. We may read the newspaper at breakfast because we happen to be having breakfast alone or because we do not want to talk to anyone else.

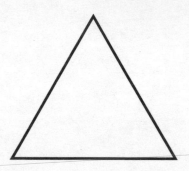

We may read the newspaper sitting in a waiting room at the dentist because there is nothing else to do. We may read a magazine sitting in an airplane because there is nothing else to do. We may watch television simply to occupy the time when we do not feel like doing anything else.

AWARENESS

Even if you are looking at the information as a distraction or as a way of filling time, you could claim that this is an exercise in 'awareness' of the world around you. You look at the television news or read the newspaper in order to be aware of what is going on. This allows you to take part in

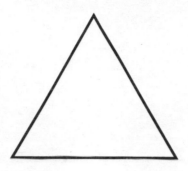

conversations on that topic or initiate such conversations.

If you are about to travel, this awareness may
indicate to you that an airport strike is planned
for your departure date. This has happened to me.
This awareness may indicate to you that there
is political turmoil in the country you plan
to visit.

A general awareness of what is going on in the
world around you is part of life. You need it.
Unfortunately, you may have to spend rather a
large amount of time looking at information in
order to find the occasional things that do matter to
you. Perhaps there is a television programme, or a

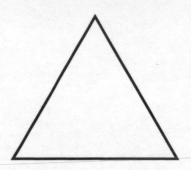

newspaper, that indicates: 'These are the things you really do need to know this week.'

So we might spend hours every week looking at a lot of information just in case there is something valuable that we need to know.

INTEREST

There are matters of interest in the material you are reading. You may be interested to read about the man who was so fat that they had to knock down part of the front of his house to get him out of bed. You may be interested to read about the wife who divorced her husband because he had lied about his

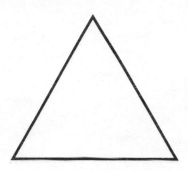

age. He had said he was ninety-five years old and he was actually only sixty-five.

There is interest in a story that starts and you want to see how it ends. This is intrinsic interest. This is 'storyline interest'.

GENERAL INTEREST

There are matters of general interest that do not relate directly to your own affairs. You may be interested to hear about a report that claims that one in four women around the world are beaten by their husbands. Are you missing out? You may be interested to hear that in Russia 85,000 women a

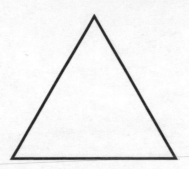

year are killed by their husbands or partners. You may well choose to doubt this.

You may be interested to hear about a species of frog in Australia that eats its own fertilised eggs, and the young develop in its stomach and jump out of its mouth when they are ready.

SPECIFIC INTEREST

If you work in the financial world, you are going to be interested in stock market reports. You are going to be interested in statements both by pundits and also by officials about the present and future state of the economy.

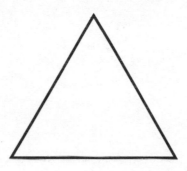

If you are concerned about your health, you are going to be interested in little snippets of information. The Finns may claim that drinking too much coffee increases the chance of arthritis. Another report may show that drinking tea reduces the chance of getting Alzheimer's by forty-five per cent. You may choose not to believe these reports without knowing the full background.

If you are interested in motor cars, you will notice the news about the Tata car that is priced at two thousand dollars. You may be interested in new hybrid cars that use hydrogen.

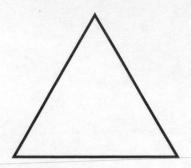

BROWSE AND SCAN

Many of the above uses of information can come under the heading of 'browse and scan'. How much of this you actually do and how much you need to do is a matter of personal preference. The point is that even when you are really doing no more than time-filling and distracting yourself, these other activities are also taking place.

NEED AND SEARCH

This is by far the most important use of information. You need some specific information, so you set out to search for that information. You need the

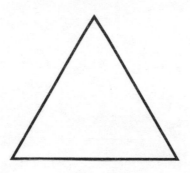

answer to a specific question, so you go and look for the answer.

This is what comes top of the list whenever we consider the use and value of information.

A person who stops you in the street to ask for directions to the train station has a specific information need. A person who consults a dictionary to find out how to spell 'insouciance' has a specific information need. A person who goes to the library to read all about Buddhism in Sri Lanka has a specific information need. A person who reads the property columns in a newspaper to get some idea of how much his home is now worth has a specific information need.

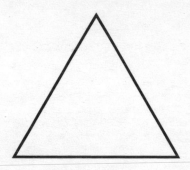

Search engines like Google and Yahoo are marvellous devices that for the first time in history allow someone to get direct and specific access to the information he or she needs. I once said, at a major university conference, that today universities are out of date. Universities were set up to make the wisdom and knowledge of the past available to students of the present. In the digital age, all needed information can be directly obtained. Perhaps universities should be teaching skills: information skills, thinking skills, people skills, management skills, etc., etc.

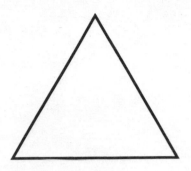

WHAT AND WHERE?

What is your information need?

What are you looking for?

The more precisely you can frame the question, the more likely you are to find an answer – and with less trouble.

There can be precise needs. I want to know if it is true that the female house spider wraps its mate up in a cocoon and then nibbles bits of the fellow when she feels hungry. Is that true?

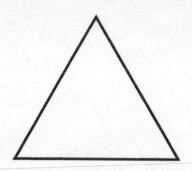

There can be much more general needs. I have bought a house with a garden and I am thinking of growing roses. Where can I find some general information on growing roses? Is it difficult? Is it expensive? Do I need to be an experienced gardener?

I occasionally get e-mails asking me to tell the sender all I know about creativity. Since I have written several books on that subject, that is a rather big demand.

'I am looking for information on where I can find information on the following matter.'

'I am looking for general information in this area.'

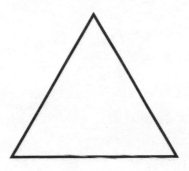

'I am looking for a specific answer to this specific question.'

CONFIRMATION

Confirmation is where you hold a specific view. You are not seeking to check it out because it is not a matter of fact. What you are really looking for is support for that view. This will not be easy to find because information is really laid out to support different views. You might need to make a general search in the subject area and then select the information that supports your view.

There is always room for general questions.

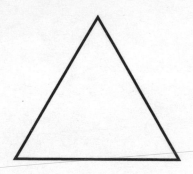

'I have heard such and such ... Is it true?'

'Someone told me ... Is it the case?'

'I half remember reading that ... Is that so?'

'I believe that ... Is that correct?'

'It is said that redheads have a much higher pain threshold than people with other colours of hair. Is this so?'

'Where can I find information to check out this point?'

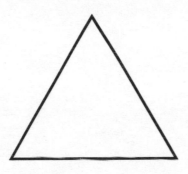

As with all questions, the more specific you can be, the more likely you are to find an answer.

'What is the general political situation in Turkmenistan?'

'What are the most common disabilities affecting older men?'

If a specific question is framed in a general way, then a lot more work will need to be done. If the questioner wants to know about a particular disability in older men, it would make sense to ask specifically about that disability rather than to hope it would come up in a general scan of disabilities.

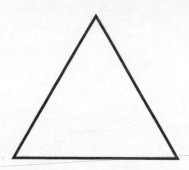

VERY SPECIFIC QUESTIONS

I need to know the time of a flight from London to Dubai that arrives in the morning. This question could be put more generally – I need to know the flight departure times for all flights from London to Dubai – and then I can make my selection to suit my exact needs.

Doctors need to frame specific questions to patients in order to help with the diagnosis. There is a general stage of asking open-ended questions. Then comes the specific stage: 'How soon after a meal does the pain come on?'

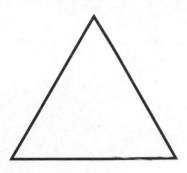

Specific questions may ask for a specific answer: 'The pain comes on about half an hour after eating.'

Specific questions may also require a yes or no answer: 'Do you ever cough up blood?'

A 'shooting question' is one with a definite answer. When you are shooting, you know what you are aiming at.

A 'fishing question' is different. When you drop a baited hook into the water, you do not know what fish or what type of fish will take the bait. This is very different from shooting at something. The question: 'What sorts of food upset you?' is different from: 'Do spicy foods upset you?'

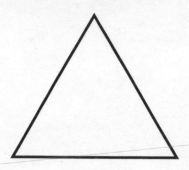

In a shooting question, there is specific information that you are seeking. In a fishing question, you only have a very general idea of the information you may obtain.

WHERE?

You can ask people.

You can ask specific people, like a travel agent, or an airline, or a doctor, or a car salesman.

You can ask people for the information, or you can ask people to suggest where you might find the information you need.

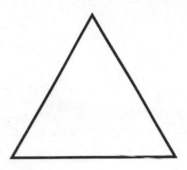

You can search the internet. You can use specific search engines like Google and Yahoo, or you can go directly to information areas relevant to your needs.

You can use a library and ask advice from the librarian.

You can go to a bookshop and buy a book on that subject. You could also subscribe to a magazine in the area of need – if there is one. You might find a magazine on rose-growing but not one on spiders.

It is not my intention here to give a full list of possible information sources.

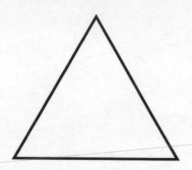

THE TRIANGLE FRAME

The purpose of the Triangle Frame is to lay out very clearly – for yourself or others to see – the purpose of looking at the information.

'Using the Triangle Frame, what is our purpose here?'

If you wish to attach a meaning to each of the three points of the triangle (which is not necessary), the three points might be:

Point 1: WHAT?   What is the purpose of our information search or scan?

PURPOSE: The Triangle Frame

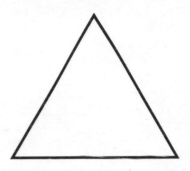

Point 2: WHY? Why do we need this information? Why is this information of value? Why will this information affect us?

Point 3: WHERE? Where should we look for this information? Are we looking in the right place?

'I want to use my Triangle Frame here. We need specific information on the number of single-parent families.'

'Triangle Frames, please. Do we know the number of unoccupied dwellings in this town?'

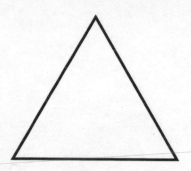

OFFERING INFORMATION

This is yet another aspect of the information purpose. There is information that you have and that you wish to place before others. You can use the Triangle Frame to signal your intention to do so.

'I want to use the Triangle Frame at this moment to put before you the results of a recent survey of the smoking habits of people under the age of sixteen years.'

'I do not know how valid this information is, but I want to use the Triangle Frame to put before you the relative number of accidents of cars of different colours.'

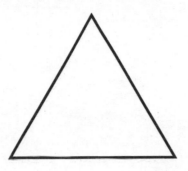

SUMMARY

The purpose of the Triangle Frame is to emphasise the huge importance of being clear and laying out the exact basis of your need for information and your interaction with the information. Most people only have a vague and general idea somewhere at the back of their minds.

Bringing that to the front of the mind and placing it before yourself, and before others, makes our use of information more effective. There is no shortage of information. We need to be clear about what we want from all that information.

2

ACCURACY

The Circle Frame

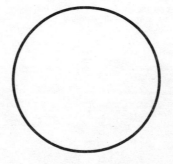

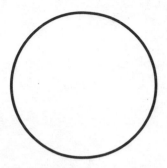

Accuracy of information is looked at through the Circle Frame. The circle represents the centre of a target, the 'bull's eye'. Accuracy depends on how well you hit that target or how far off you might be.

Accuracy of information is of vital importance if you have to rely on that information for action, belief or opinion.

It is a sobering fact to learn that fifty-six per cent of young people in the United Kingdom do not trust newspapers. This might be more expected of older people with some years of experience of newspaper inaccuracy or even dishonesty – but for young people it is more surprising.

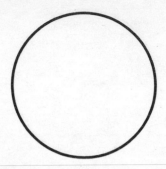

AUTHORITY

Authority is too often our only way of checking accuracy. If the source is authoritative and credible, we believe what we read or what we hear. This is what happens at university with professors and lecturers. This is what happens when your doctor tells you something. This is what happens when you access a credible website.

You believe in the basic honesty and reliability of the source.

The news part of broadcasting stations (radio and television) is reasonably accurate because it cannot afford to lose credibility. There may be some slight

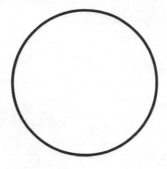

personal bias on specific occasions, but this would be the exception.

The news part of newspapers is probably equally accurate, partly because it comes from news agencies that have no need to be inaccurate.

Unfortunately, this respect for the news sections should not be extended to other sections of newspapers, which may be seriously dishonest. You need to have personal experience of this to make that accusation. Even well-respected newspapers publish biased articles. I recall one piece that did not, in my view, fairly reflect me or my work as it was extremely selective and left out relevant and positive research results in schools. It also made

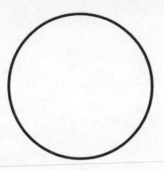

great use of personal adjectives which, in my view, did not contribute to the piece. I tend to judge newspapers not by their best pieces but by their worst, and I firmly believe newspaper editors should realise this. (Interestingly, the journalist who wrote the piece was later chosen as 'young journalist of the year'. I wonder whether their piece about me was considered by the judges...)

Authority of source has to be trusted on most occasions because we need the information and have no way of checking it out for ourselves. We may have our doubts, but there is no way we can check them out.

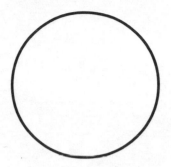

INTERNAL CHECKING

There may sometimes be internal inconsistencies in the information that is being offered. This can trigger doubts about the accuracy of the whole.

More often there is some claim or some fact that a particular reader happens to know to be wrong. This demolishes the accuracy of the whole piece and the permanent credibility of the source. This may be an over-reaction to a small error, but if, as a supplier of information, you set out to pretend accuracy, you need to be very careful indeed to preserve that reputation. You can never afford any blatant or even minor demonstration of inaccuracy.

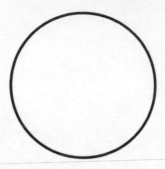

Sometimes we may not immediately know that a claim or fact is false, but there are ways of checking it out. If it proves to be false, we will have even less respect for the source that has put us through the trouble of checking out the accuracy.

COMPARATIVE ACCURACY

Sometimes you can compare two different reports of the same event or occasion. If there is a difference, then they cannot both be accurate. You may have to check even further reports to see which of the two versions is the more correct. They may, of course, both be inadequate.

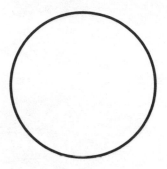

Comparing different sources is a standard way of checking for accuracy. Unfortunately, in most situations there are not alternative reports to compare.

ADEQUATE ACCURACY

If you have to take action or make a decision, you have to work with the best information you can get. Usually it is not possible to delay action or decision until you are fully satisfied with the accuracy of the information.

So we often have to make assessments regarding the adequacy of the accuracy of the information. We assess whether, on the whole, the information is accurate,

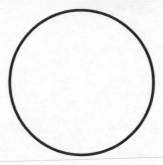

even though there may be minor errors. Such assessments are not easy but may have to be made.

DOUBTS

There are different sorts of doubt. There can be doubt expressed in the information itself. Users are urged to be cautious in the use of the information and to seek to check it out for themselves.

The user of the information can have doubts and may express these doubts to himself or herself or to others, say at a meeting. Doubts do not themselves destroy the validity of the information, but suggest caution in its use.

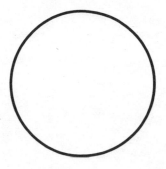

Attempts may be made to check out the accuracy of information. Rarely can this be done directly, but using other sources a comparison can be made.

Above all, doubts need to be clearly underlined.

THE CIRCLE FRAME

As a practical matter, it may be easier to refer to the 'Circle Frame' rather than the 'Circular Frame' because there are contexts in which 'circular' could have another meaning. In general, both are acceptable.

The purpose of the Circle Frame is to focus directly on the accuracy of the information. If we are

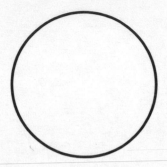

going to take the information into account, and if we are going to act on the information, the accuracy of that information is of the highest importance.

Information that is not accurate is at best misleading and at worst very dangerous.

'I want to use the Circle Frame on those statistics about exercise and health.'

'Circle Frame that point, will you.'

'We need to Circle Frame that insinuation because it could make all the difference to the promotion.'

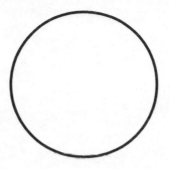

'Our strategy is going to be based on the taste differences between men and women. We really must Circle Frame the research about this taste difference. Will you do that?'

The Circle Frame can be used to pinpoint the importance of some piece of information and the need to check it out.

The Circle Frame can be used to indicate an area of existing doubt and to let others know about this doubt.

The Circle Frame can be used to invite investigation of an area in order to collect accurate information.

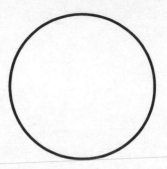

The Circle Frame can be used to judge the accuracy of information sources.

SUMMARY

The Circle Frame invites us to direct our attention specifically to the accuracy of the information at which we are looking. The value of that information depends directly on the accuracy assessment.

We often take accuracy too easily for granted. This is because we trust the sources, such as newspapers, and also because it would be very difficult to check things out all the time. For the practical purposes of action, we are too ready

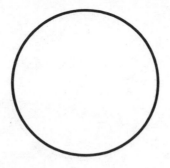

to accept the accuracy of the information we need.

The Circle Frame is an invitation to ourselves and to others to look directly at the fundamental accuracy of information.

3

POINT OF VIEW

The Square Frame

In a square, all sides are exactly equal. That is the definition of a square. There may not be many situations where there are four sides to an issue, but if there were, they would all be treated equally. The square also suggests that it is possible to approach an issue from any side.

There is an overlap between the accuracy frame (Circle) and the view frame (Square). If a situation is presented in a biased way, then that is not accurate. If only one side of the picture is given, then that is not accurate. At the same time, a report may accurately present just one side of the picture.

For various practical reasons, there is a need to have a frame that notes the point of view of the

information. No matter how much we may assume neutrality, it is useful to have a frame that directs our attention to the point of view that is being used.

PERSUASION

There is a lot of information that never claims to be neutral. Such information is designed to be one-sided, biased and persuasive.

An advertisement for a motor car does not claim accurately to list all the rival cars, but seeks to extol the virtues of the brand that is advertised. All advertising is designed to be persuasive and not neutral. Otherwise it would be useless as advertising.

A lawyer in court, in the adversarial system, takes a deliberately biased point of view. That is the nature of that system – as distinct from an exploratory system.

A political speech before an election, and even after, is designed to be persuasive. A political attack on an opponent is not intended to be a balanced assessment. All the scandals and shortcomings are noted – the achievements are not.

Because persuasive material does not claim to be neutral, it is not treated as such. It does, however, need to be accurate in its claims, no matter how one-sided.

DIFFICULTY OF BALANCE

It is difficult to write a balanced report, because the whole of education seeks to get students to take a one-sided view both in their essays and in debates. You are supposed to make a point and come to a conclusion. To do that, you have to select and fit together the facts that go to make up your chosen story.

Story-telling is important to all parts of the media. It is believed, probably correctly, that only stories are interesting – accurate facts are not. Story-telling demands a single point of view, not multiple points of view.

You can examine the situation and then put the pieces together to form a story that seems to arise from the situation itself.

More often, newspapers have a story firmly in mind before they even view the situation. Then they look at the situation through the story they want to write and select only those pieces that fit their predetermined story. This has been my personal experience. If the pieces do not fit or even threaten to weaken the story, then they are simply ignored and left out. After all, the reader has no way of knowing what has been left out.

Writers are often seen to be successful if the reader can take away from the piece some single conclusion

or story. To go away with a balanced view is unnatural, difficult and boring. In the animal world you are either food for someone else or you see food for yourself – there is not much in between.

THE USE OF ADJECTIVES

Always look out for the use of adjectives in a press piece. Adjectives are almost never objective. They reflect the personal opinion and attitude of the writer.

Adjectives like 'selfish', 'pompous', 'dismissive', 'snide', 'crafty', 'greedy', boastful', etc., etc., are all flavoured opinions that may or may not be based

on anything concrete. Facts can stand for themselves but adjectives cannot. Adjectives depend on the writer putting them forward as if they were verifiable facts – when they may depend on no more than the indigestion or the envy of the writer. So when you read this sort of piece, count the 'adjective score' and then you can see how reliable that source may be.

POINT OF VIEW

The police and social workers may see binge drinking amongst youngsters as a problem. It leads to motor accidents, to fights, to violence, to muggings, etc. The owners of bars and makers of

the drinks see binge drinking as an unfortunate excess of a fundamentally good thing. There are more profits if people drink more. You can be against excess and abuse without being against the fundamental process. We do not forbid car driving because there are road deaths.

Many people are against divorce. People in a difficult marriage welcome the opportunity of divorce.

Information may be written from one point of view because the writer can only have that point of view. This is not intended to be persuasive or advertising, but the effect is the same. Of course, the single view may be entirely negative, and that is different from advertising – it may be a sort of

negative advertising. Some people in Russia look back on the old days of the Soviet Union with nostalgia and regret that those days are no more. Others welcome the changes.

Figuring out that information may be provided from only one point of view is part of the operation of the square frame. Identifying what that point of view may be is also part of that frame.

Information from a particular point of view is not necessarily inaccurate (except for its one-sided and incomplete nature) or unusable. Once you have determined its nature, then the information can have its uses.

THE POWER OF BALANCE

A balanced piece is very rare and very powerful, because the reader feels that he or she is being put in the observer seat and is not being lectured at.

Perception has to work by coming to a conclusion as quickly as possible and then filling in the details later. This quick conclusion provides the framework for looking further into the matter. If it were not for this, animals would have a very hard time. When you see a predator approaching, you have to jump to a conclusion as quickly as you can. You cannot carry out a detailed assessment to see if the predator is hungry or limping, etc. The predator is not going to wait for you to do so.

In the same way, the mind tends to jump to a perceptual conclusion (good guy or bad guy) as soon as possible, and then seeks to fill in the details as seen through this initial perception.

Can you imagine a newspaper piece that starts: 'This piece is written by Gemma Soackes, who does not like the way they treat women in Tsa Tsa Land ...'?

In some cultures, like the Zulu culture, the men wave spears and wear leopardskin leggings on tribal occasions. They may be very fierce, but in the background the women run things and make all the decisions. Things are not always what they seem to a superficial reporter.

ALTERNATIVE VIEWS FROM THE SAME POINT

This is an extremely important role for the square frame. Up until this point we have considered different points of view, bias, neutrality, etc. Here we consider the same point of view but with an alternative view.

Here the reader (or listener) chooses to look at the available information in alternative ways. The attempt is to see things differently from the same point of view.

More and more corporations are simply collecting information and putting it all into their computers.

The computers then analyse the information, and make the decisions and set the strategy for the corporation. This growing habit is extremely dangerous.

There is a need to look at the information in different ways. Computers cannot do this, so the corporation remains locked in the old concepts. Only humans can choose to look at the information in different ways.

Research shows that people who smoke a lot of cannabis have an increased chance of developing schizophrenia. So cannabis is seen as a causative agent. Looked at differently, it may be that those with a schizophrenic tendency enjoy cannabis

more and so smoke more. Later this schizophrenic tendency becomes manifest as schizophrenia.

Someone once remarked to me that since a lot of brilliant people come out of Harvard University, the teaching techniques must be very good. I suggested that if a lot of brilliant people went into an archway, then a lot of brilliant people would come out of that archway – which had contributed little.

It is always assumed that the spikes on desert cacti are to stop animals eating the cacti. This may not be so. The small spikes also keep the boundary layer of air next to the plant stationary so that there is less loss of water through transpiration, evaporation, etc.

Looking at data in different and lateral ways is going to become more and more important as the habit of feeding all information into computers grows.

THE SQUARE FRAME

The Square Frame is really asking us to pay attention to the degree of bias or neutrality in the information. Is the information objective or subjective? We may not be able to do much about it, but noticing the bias can affect the way we use the information.

We may also choose not to use a source that is consistently one-sided.

The Square Frame also suggests that we ourselves can choose to look at the information in a different way (from another side of the square).

'There is the data and there is the conclusion. If you use your Square Frame, you can look at it in a different way and reach a different conclusion.'

'Is this the only way of viewing the data?'

'This report seems very balanced. Use your Square Frame and see if you detect bias.'

'My Square Frame tells me this information is very one-sided. The practical question is whether we can make use of it at all.'

'Before jumping to conclusions, let us Square Frame this report.'

'My Square Frame tells me this is very one-sided. But I cannot see what the other side could be.'

SUMMARY

Looking at information in different ways is going to become more and more important as we get used to putting information into a computer and abiding by the analysis of that computer.

It may seem a waste of time to assess information for neutrality when neutrality is so rarely the case.

At the same time, it is useful and important to spell out the nature and strength of any bias. Without such a clarification it is difficult and dangerous to use that information.

If the Square Frame became a regular reader habit, then perhaps newspaper editors would make more effort to provide balanced views – difficult as that may be. Otherwise, readers might shift to publications that did provide more balanced views.

INTEREST

The Heart Frame

Matters of the heart are always of great interest to the person owning that particular heart. They are usually of interest to other people too. So the heart-shaped frame symbolises 'interest'. It is enough to talk about the 'Heart Frame'; there is no need to repeat 'heart-shaped frame'.

In a sense, interest is useless – but it is the most fascinating aspect of information. Interest is not the opposite of need, but it is very different.

Interest is attractive and appealing. Something you pick up out of interest enters your memory and may be of great use later – but you do not pick it up for its usefulness.

GENERAL INTEREST

You may be interested to read that the population of Nigeria is 140 million people. You may have thought it to be about 40 million. You are surprised, and that is a form of interest. This knowledge also adds to your general education.

Surprise is always a good source of interest. Finding out something that is contrary to your existing knowledge is always both interesting and useful. Finding out something you did not know at all is also interesting.

Reading that the hobby of the President of Ireland is knitting is of interest. Learning that the last president was also a woman is of interest. Maybe it

makes more sense to have a woman president. That way the men do not get jealous of each other.

Learning about the success of the social networking sites on the internet is both surprising and interesting. Any powerful phenomenon is always interesting.

ADDITION

This is another source of interest. You know something about a subject, and what you read adds to that knowledge. You may know something about sharks. Then you read about the mating habits of sharks, and this is interesting because it adds on to your existing knowledge. This new knowledge may

have no practical value at all – either now or in the future.

For some people, celebrities are always a source of interest. They are rather like the Greek gods of old. People were always fascinated by the domestic and romantic behaviour of these gods. So once a celebrity is established as a point of interest, even the slightest bit of news is of interest. Who is going out with whom? What is their new baby called? Who has split up with whom? Does she really drink a lot of whisky?

Contradiction of your existing knowledge is also a source of interest, but this comes under 'surprise' as described above.

RESEARCH

Research results are always of interest because it is assumed that they are authoritative. Research that suggests that happy people are fat and that worriers are thin is of interest both to fat people and to thin people – and to everyone else.

Research that claims to show that some of the happiest people in the world live on the island of Malta is interesting, even if you wonder how that figure was obtained.

Research that shows that drinking red wine makes you live longer is of great interest, because most people do want to live longer.

Research that relates directly to you as a human being is of more interest than research on the life history of rats.

It is very interesting to learn that today in the USA youngsters actually spend more time on the internet than watching television. It may be less interesting, to most people, to learn that many newspaper circulations are declining because of a shift of attention to television news and advertising revenue to the internet.

SPECIAL INTEREST

You are planning a holiday in the Maldives, so anything at all about these islands is of great interest to you.

Your hobby is homing pigeons, so anything about this subject is of special interest.

You are a football fanatic, so any news, gossip or information of any sort about your favoured team (and even football in general) is of great interest to you.

You are in the construction business, so any information about new technology or new regulations is of very direct interest to you.

This is a situation where interest and need coincide.

You have a general interest in computers and IT, though this is not a professional interest. New developments and new trends in this area become of interest to you.

You need to buy a new car. For the moment, all matters relating to different models are of interest. This information will cease to be of interest once you have bought the car. Indeed, you may come to avoid such information in case you find out you have made a mistake in your purchase of a particular model.

You have to write a school essay on traffic lights.

Suddenly the positioning and effectiveness of the traffic lights in your town becomes of great interest.

While 'general interest' does not need the concept of relevance, 'special interest' is directly based on relevance.

NOTE-TAKING

This is a tedious suggestion and not many people will want to do it. The idea is that when you have read through an article or substantial piece of information, you should take a moment to note down, as briefly as you wish, what you have found interesting in that piece. Writing this down

physically is much more valuable than just pausing and making a mental note of what you would have written down if you had bothered.

It is not so much the note-taking that is valuable. But knowing that you will have to note something down makes you read the piece much more carefully and with greater attention to what might be of interest in the piece.

MINING

In a diamond mine you are looking for diamonds. In a gold mine you are looking for gold. In the same

way, you can set out to 'mine' a piece of information for its interest value.

This process is similar to the one mentioned under the 'purpose' frame. You can walk down the street and wait for things to catch your attention. Or you could deliberately direct your attention to some aspect or another.

In exactly the same way, we can mine information for interest. We can wait for interest to catch our attention, or we can direct our attention. For example, we could direct our attention to the economic impact of what we are reading.

You could try the exercise of taking a really dull article and setting yourself the task of mining or extracting interest from it. It is difficult at first, but becomes easier with practice.

THE HEART FRAME

'Using the Heart Frame, I find it very interesting that young people are becoming more interested in religion.'

'I know that this report seems to be very dull. But I want you all to use your Heart Frames and report back to me on what you find interesting.'

'Using the Heart Frame is all very well, but we still need practical information in order to design our products.'

'Please use your Heart Frame and go through this all over again. I do not want us to miss anything.'

'He is not very good with the Heart Frame. He does not notice anything unless it hits him between the eyes.'

'Heart frames, everyone, please.'

People do not need to be encouraged to notice matters of great interest and importance. The purpose of the Heart Frame is to encourage people

to make more effort to note matters of interest when these are not quite so obvious. You could call it 'reading between the lines'. This phrase has exactly the same meaning, but is much more cumbersome to use.

SUMMARY

When we are using information to answer some need, then that need is strong enough to search the information. There is more, however, in information than the satisfaction of the need of the moment. The Heart Frame directs attention to matters of interest.

INTEREST: The Heart Frame

There may be matters of general interest and there may be matters of special interest that are related to something we are doing or about to do.

'Interest' may seem an intangible area, but it is a very important one. Over time, a sensitivity to interest builds up a large store of background information that will become useful in many situations.

5

VALUE

The Diamond Frame

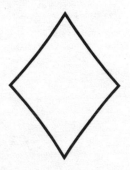

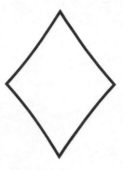

Diamonds are a symbol of value. So the diamond-shaped frame indicates a value scan: 'What is the value of this information?'

There is an obvious overlap between need, value and interest, but they also need to be separated.

Information that answers a question or fulfils a need is obviously of value.

Something that is of interest is also of value. This applies even more to special interest.

The value frame would tend to be used at the end – after the use of the other frames. What has been the value in this information?

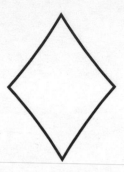

NEED SATISFACTION

You need some particular information, such as the departure time of the last flight to Australia. You get that definite information from a reliable source. Your need has been met. You are satisfied.

You need some information about the latest treatment for arthritis. You ask your doctor. You get that information. You are not totally happy that your local doctor is really up to date, so you do a search on the internet and find that your doctor was right.

You are looking for a partner. You find one on an internet dating site.

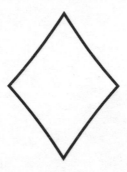

You ask yourself the question: has this information satisfied my need?

There are some needs that are open-ended. If you need information on the economy of Bolivia, you might find very good information in *The Economist* magazine, but there may be more. There is no limit to the information that would still be of value to you. There is a need, however, to be practical.

QUESTION ANSWERED

A definite question is even more specific than a need. You frame the question very carefully and

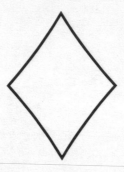

then you assess whether the information has indeed answered your question.

The question may be in two parts. First, where do I find the information to answer this question of mine? Then you ask the question of the indicated information source.

There may still be doubts. You may feel that the question has not been fully answered. You may have doubts about the credibility of the answer. That is where your value assessment can come in.

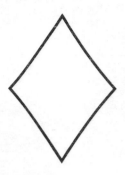

INTEREST VALUE

Something of interest always has some value, even if it does not answer a need of the moment. The interest can be enjoyable – which is a value in itself. The interest can add to your general store of knowledge – which may be of value at some point in the future.

With 'special interests' that have some relevance to some activity of yours both now and in the future, there is a more obvious value. Information about a country you are due to visit is of value.

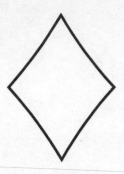

CONFIRMATION VALUE

Information that supports and confirms your view on a subject is of great value even if nothing new is added. The value lies in increasing the confidence with which you hold the view and adding to your arguments when seeking to persuade others of your view.

DISAGREEMENT VALUE

When the information you access disagrees with your view and does not confirm it, what is the value? The value is to show that there is another point of view. There is also value in examining

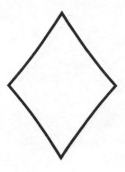

the strengths and weaknesses of this other point of view. That may allow you to defend your point of view and attack the other.

It is also possible that you may actually be persuaded to drop your own point of view to take up the new one. That is a real value. If you win an argument you do not gain much, but if you lose an argument you gain a lot.

OPPORTUNITY

The information may hint at a new opportunity, or may lay out a new opportunity for either business activities or more personal activities. The opportunity

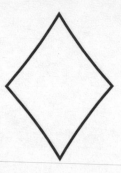

may only be suggested and will need to be followed up to get more details. Nevertheless, a direction of enquiry can be set.

Information may suggest that something you possess may be of far greater value than you realised. As a student I once sold a motor car for five pounds. A few years later that make, and that year (1935), was selling for £250,000 (though probably in better condition than mine).

Information may let you know of a very good discount offer for a cruise to the Caribbean.

You may have been searching for information related to a possible opportunity, or you may come

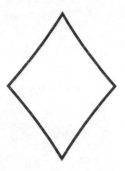

across such information by chance in the course of reading or listening.

AWARENESS OF THE WORLD AROUND US

This is always a real value. To be aware that there are no transport strikes pending is of value. To be aware that there has been no change in the exchange rate is of value. Information indicating that there has been no change is always of value if there might have been a change that could have affected you.

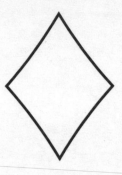

Looking at the news on television has a value even if almost all the news is about trouble in other parts of the world.

In addition to the value of 'protective awareness' and also 'opportunity awareness', there is a further value. If you are aware of what is going on, you can take part in more conversations and even initiate conversations relating to happenings in the world, generally or locally.

Awareness is a real value even if we do not appreciate it at the time. The difficulty is knowing where to draw the line. Every little bit more of awareness has a potential value. You can read a dozen newspapers on this basis, or watch television

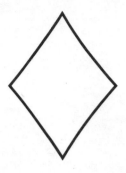

for hours. You have to decide that really important matters will be widely reported and that therefore even a short time devoted to 'awareness' will be sufficient – like watching the news once a day.

ENRICHMENT

Everyone knows something about a lot of things. Information enriches the existing knowledge whether we are conscious of this or not. This is a value of information but not one strong enough to encourage us to read all information because of this possibility of enrichment. Again there is a need to be practical.

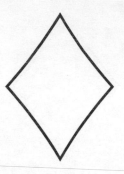

NOTE-TAKING

As with 'interest', it might be useful at the end of reading or otherwise accessing information to make a note of 'What has been the value here?' It is not suggested that you do this for both interest and value. It might be enough to ask yourself that question in definite ways:

'What has been the value here?'

'Has the information answered my needs and questions?'

'What extra value has the information provided?'

'In what way am I better informed?'

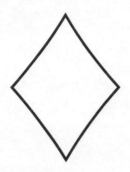

SIX VALUE MEDALS

In my book *The Six Value Medals*, I discuss six different types of value. This is to make each type easier to recognise. There are the following values:

Gold Medal: values that are human values and apply directly to people. There are both positive (appreciation, etc.) and negative (humiliation, etc.) values.

Silver Medal: values that apply to the organisation, whether business, family, group, etc. These might include profits, market share, brand image, etc. Again, there are both positive and negative values.

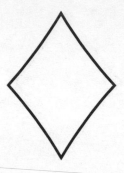

Steel Medal: these are direct quality values (both positive and negative). How does this value impact on quality?

Glass Medal: this is for innovation and creative values. What is new here?

Wood Medal: ecology values in the broadest sense. Not just nature, but the world around.

Brass Medal: perceptual values. How will this be perceived?

You could include some of the medals in the assessment value.

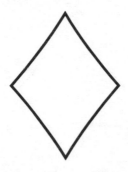

THE DIAMOND FRAME

'On with the Diamond Frame. What is the direct value of this new information?'

'I want to summarise with the Diamond Frame. I see the value of this information as follows ...'

'I do not see that as a real value. You may need to polish your Diamond Frame.'

'Let's discuss the values here. There may be many different values. Diamond Frames, please.'

'The value may seem obvious, but I feel that some further scanning through the Diamond Frame will reveal more than what is obvious.'

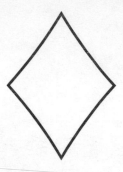

The importance of values may be subjective, but the existence of values is not. Your Diamond Frame should reveal all possible values – even ones you do not give much importance to.

SUMMARY

The Diamond Frame is a sort of summary and overview: 'What has been the value of this information?' There are different types of value and different levels of value. The Diamond Frame is all about clarification of these values through direct attention. Even if a value has been seen through another frame, it can be seen again with the Diamond Frame.

6

OUTCOME

The Slab Frame

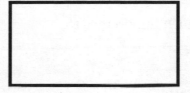

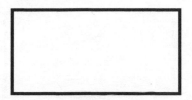

What do we put on the slab at the end? What is the outcome? What is the conclusion? The slab represents a platform on which something is to be placed and exhibited.

'Are we agreed on the conclusion?'

'What is my personal conclusion?'

It may be that time has been wasted looking at unreliable information of very little value. It may be that our needs have been exactly satisfied. It may be that there has been a lot of very useful extra information.

With the Slab Frame we lay out our conclusions.

Have our information needs been satisfied? How have they been satisfied? Do we need further information? Are we happy with the accuracy of the information? Do any further questions arise?

What is the overall value of the information? What is the value directly related to our needs? What is the extra value? Have new directions of enquiry been opened up? What is the impact of the value obtained from the information? How does this value influence our actions, our strategy, our plans, our problem-solving, etc?

What matters of interest have been noted in the information? Why are these matters of interest? Do

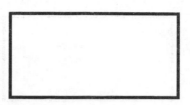

we need to do anything further about these matters of interest?

These questions need to be answered in a clear way. The whole purpose of the Six Frames is to move towards clarity. This means being able to direct attention to one thing at a time and one thing after another – instead of having everything jumbled up together.

NEXT STEP

What is the next step? Do we need further information? Do we need to take action on the basis of the information we now have?

113

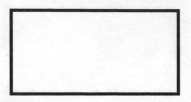

If the information has caused us to change our minds, what do we do about that? In what way does that change impact on our thinking and our strategy? Do we need to let other people know about this change?

SO WHAT?

The information scan has been useful, but it has not changed our thinking in any way. So, have we wasted our time? Reassurance has a high value. If the information has confirmed that our thinking is on the right track, this is both important and useful.

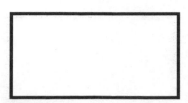

INFORMATION REPORT

You could write an information report for yourself and for others. Reports from different people can be compared. Such reports would go through each of the Six Frames with comments under each frame.

Obviously this would not be done for every piece of information, but it could be done for serious reports or information that is judged to be very relevant.

The absorption of information is so very important for thinking that we need to take it seriously.

Everyone knows the importance of information. We have, however, done very little about how we use this information and the impact of this information.

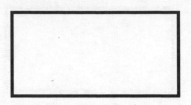

COMPUTERS

We are getting used to putting all our information into a computer and then letting the computer analyse that information. This is a growing danger.

The matters covered by the Six Frames cannot easily be done by computer. A computer cannot assess accuracy, interest, neutrality or value. All these involve the human interface.

So the more we make use of computers for information, the greater the need for these frames.

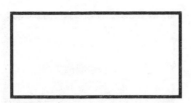

THE SLAB FRAME

'What have you got to put on the slab?'

'Using the Slab Frame, what are our immediate conclusions?'

'Has this information been useful? What is the slab outcome?'

'Everyone use your Slab Frame. Then we can compare the conclusions.'

'We have put a lot of effort and money into this. What do we see with the Slab Frame?'

'I feel my Slab Frame conclusion is very different from yours. Let us discuss the differences.'

SUMMARY

The Slab Frame is for the outcome and conclusion. It requires a deliberate effort to lay out the conclusion on the slab for yourself and others to see. It is no longer enough to assume that everyone faced with the same information comes to the same conclusion. There is a need to spell out the conclusion in a clear and deliberate manner. To do this we have to think about it. That is what matters.

SUMMARY

We cannot live without information. There is information we really need. Then there is information that affects us.

You may have decided where you want to go on holiday and you then look for the specific information you need. Alternatively, you may see an advertisement for a holiday destination you have never considered and begin to think of going to this new destination.

We are surrounded by information. The value, accuracy and interest of this information may vary considerably.

The Six Frames laid out in this book and the strong symbols of the six shapes allow us to be more deliberate about the way we choose to look at information. We can consciously prepare our minds to notice different aspects of the information. This enables us to get far more value from the information.

The frames can be used by an individual as he or she looks at information. The frames can be used as a language code between two people or in a group discussion. They provide a simple shorthand for directing attention or suggesting that attention may be directed to one particular aspect of the information.

TRUTH PASTE

We all know what toothpaste is supposed to do. It is supposed to keep the teeth white and gleaming. In addition, it might also provide care for the gums.

What about 'truth paste'?

Very few people set out to be dishonest by lying or saying things they know to be untrue.

Most people believe that what they are saying is not deliberately untrue. They may feel that it is completely true, or true enough, or as true as can be ascertained.

The way we treat things so that they appear true to ourselves and to others is known as 'truth paste'.

It seems that for women, three things have the same effect. They all raise a chemical called phenylethylamine in the blood. The three things are chocolate, shopping and falling in love.

For men, it seems that the three things are curry, making money and looking at *Playboy* magazine. All these cause activity in the pleasure centre in the brain.

These effects have been reported as serious research. Basing something upon research is part of truth paste. There may be no doubt that the research has taken place, but unless you read the research report in detail, you do not know how the research was carried out. Were these the things that had more effect than any other things? How many different things were tried out? Did most people react in the same way?

In another research report, young men and young women were placed opposite each other at a table. They looked at each other for five minutes without saying a word. Three years later, 90 per cent of the couples were married.

Were the couples picked randomly from the population? Were the couples picked from a university or other closed group? If the couples were picked from a closed group, then the staring exercise might have provided the starting point for getting to know each other better. If the couples were not from a closed group, then the result is even more astonishing.

Exaggeration is a common form of truth paste.

Adjectives are nearly always a form of truth paste. Adjectives are almost always subjective. If you say something is yellow, then this can be tested with a spectrometer. But if you say that something is beautiful, attractive, subtle, outrageous, flashy, cheap-looking, then you are merely expressing your opinion. You can count the adjectives in a piece of journalism to know how much truth paste is being used. What is boring to one person may be fascinating to another.

There is nothing wrong with subjective opinions. Some people like parsnips, and others do not. The problem only arises when, through the use of adjectives, a subjective opinion is put forward as fact. This is truth paste of the worst kind.

Quoting eminent figures or authorities is another form of truth paste. Sometimes there is credibility in the experience of the person quoted. At other times it is just celebrity with no special credibility.

Advertising has to depend on truth paste. The reader of the advertisement has to believe it to be true if he or she is going to act on the advertisement at some time. Yet very few of the claims put forward can actually be tested.

Truth paste has a value. We could not operate without truth paste. We need to believe that something is reasonably true even if it has not really been proven.

The important point is to develop the concept of truth paste so that, with the help of the appropriate frame, we can tell when it is being used.

ABOUT THE AUTHOR

Edward de Bono is the leading authority in the field of creative thinking and the direct teaching of thinking as a skill. While there are thousands of people writing software for computers, Edward de Bono is the pioneer in writing software for the human brain.

From an understanding of how the human brain works as a self-organising information system, he derived the formal creative tools of lateral thinking. He is also the originator of 'parallel thinking' and the Six Thinking Hats. His tools for perceptual thinking (CoRT and DATT) are widely used in both schools and business.

Edward de Bono's instruction in thinking has been sought by many of the leading corporations in the world, such as IBM, Microsoft, Prudential, BT (UK), NTT (Japan), Nokia (Finland) and Siemens (Germany). The Australian national cricket team also sought his help and became the most successful cricket team in history.

A group of academics in South Africa included Dr de Bono as one of the 250 people who had most influenced humanity in the whole course of history. A leading Austrian business journal chose him as one of the 20 visionaries alive today. The leading consultancy company Accenture named him as one of the 50 most influential current business thinkers.

Edward de Bono's methods are simple but powerful. The use of just one method produced 21,000 ideas for a steel company in one afternoon. He has taught thinking to Nobel Prize winners and to young people with Down's syndrome.

Edward de Bono holds an MD (Malta), MA (Oxford), DPhil (Oxford), PhD (Cambridge), DDes (RMIT) and LLD (Dundee). He has had faculty appointments at the universities of Oxford, Cambridge, London and Harvard and was a Rhodes

Scholar at Oxford. He has written more than 70 books with translations into 40 languages and has been invited to lecture in 58 countries.

The Edward de Bono Foundation is concerned with the teaching of constructive thinking in Education and Management. For further information contact:

The Edward de Bono Foundation
PO Box 2397
Dublin 8
Ireland
Tel: +353 1 8250466
Email: debono@iol.ie
Website: www.edwarddebonofoundation.com

The Six Value Medals

Whether as an individual, a business executive or a director you are looking to be the best, this is the book that could improve your company, your career – and your life.

Values are central to everything: the purpose of any business or government organisation is to deliver value, and increasingly we seek this in our personal lives as well. Yet values are vague and intangible. In this ground-breaking book, Edward de Bono reveals an exciting but simple framework for individuals and business leaders alike for making creative, effective decisions, based on embracing key values – the focus of the twenty-first century.

Offering sound advice on decision making and better thinking practice, *The Six Value Medals* thwarts traditional thinking habits, demonstrates how you can deal with values in a much more definite way and enables you to highlight your strengths while pinpointing areas for improvement, helping you and your company become more successful.

It's time to start using the Six Value Medals!

H+ (Plus) A New Religion?

Edward de Bono has revolutionised the way we think. And now he's about to change the way we live our lives ...

In this groundbreaking, thought-provoking book, Edward de Bono offers us a new way of living based on an entirely positive way of life. In H+ (Plus) he provides a framework for happiness through daily acts of help or contribution. Whether this is offering other people something to laugh at or helping an elderly person cross the road, these altruistic acts lead to a sense of achievement, and from achievement comes self-esteem and a belief in oneself.

Discover the secret to leading a fuller, happier, healthier, more positive way of life.

How to Have Creative Ideas

In *How to Have Creative Ideas*, Edward de Bono outlines 62 different games and exercises, using random words as a provocation to encourage creativity and lateral thinking.

Simple, practical and fun, this book is for anyone who wants to have great ideas.

☐ **How to Have a Beautiful Mind**	9780091894603	£8.99
☐ **The Six Value Medals**	9780091894597	£8.99
☐ **H+ (Plus) A New Religion?**	9780091910471	£6.99
☐ **How to Have Creative Ideas**	9780091910488	£8.99

FREE POSTAGE AND PACKING
Overseas customers allow £2.00 per paperback.

BY PHONE: 01624 677237

BY POST: Random House Books
c/o Bookpost, PO Box 29, Douglas,
Isle of Man, IM99 1BQ

BY FAX: 01624 670923

BY EMAIL: bookshop@enterprise.net

Cheques (payable to Bookpost) and credit cards accepted.
Prices and availability subject to change without notice.
Allow 28 days for delivery.

When placing your order, please mention if you do not wish
to receive any additional information.

www.rbooks.co.uk